To my beautiful family, you are my greatest teachers.

A wonderful story about Evie's five secrets of gratitude, connection, kindness, embracing our uniqueness and presence.

This book will stimulate conversation in all the family helping everyone live a more grounded, loving life!

This is Evie!

Evie's a real cool girl who loves herself!

It really is the only way to live in perfect health!

Come and see how Evie enjoys life to the max.

She'll teach you her secrets as we follow her tracks!

Evie wakes up in the morning with a stretch and a smile.

She says "thank you" to her bed and dresses in style!

Evie looks out the window and says "Good morning world!"

"Gratitude is the best way to start the day, haven't you heard?"

Gratitude means to give thanks for what you have,

to feel it in your heart and not just by halves!

When you are grateful the universe knows to send you more!

This simple trick really opens up life's biggest doors.

As Evie skips to the kitchen,

she gives thanks for her body!

It helps her to run, skip, dance, even pet her dog

Scotty!

Give gratitude a try! It will transform your day!

You'll see so many great things that don't require

you to pay!

It's breakfast time now. Evie has some fruit and nuts.

She drinks up her water – no ifs or buts!

Then Evie asks where her food comes from.

"It comes from the earth" says Evie's mom!

They talk about farms which grow fruit and veg.

They talk about hens who lay all the eggs!

They find out about factories where donuts are made and how they put fillings into bars – it's pureed!

This is Evie's second secret; **be connected to everything** including your food.

When you pay close attention you'll see how it affects your mood!

The truth is no foods are good or bad!

They just affect our bodies differently and some make our tummies feel sad!

When Evie has food that comes from the earth she's full of energy and feels really happy!

But too many sweets can make her feel tired and snappy!

After breakfast Evie skips to the garden.

She trips over her cat Lily and says "I beg your pardon!"

Evie pets her cat and is loving and **kind,**

This is the third secret to creating a calm mind.

You see it's always best to be kind to others.

When we are nasty or mean everyone suffers!

It feels better for us to share, be caring and loving.

There's no room for kindness if we are pushing or shoving!

Evie's family joins her in the garden to play.

It's important to make it a part of every day!

When we play it's fun and makes us light up with joy.

There's lots to discover - even in the soil!

Having fun and doing what makes you feel good too.

Is Evie's fourth secret – **to be uniquely you!**

Each one of us have a unique set of talents, that work in flow to create universal balance!

The key to discovering what your talents are is to give things a try, maybe even the guitar!

Evie's talents are art and playing trombone. In the future she dreams of having a gallery of her own!

You'll know if you like it because it will feel good inside.

Remember feelings are messengers to act as our guide!

This leads us to Evie's final secret - **to be present every day.**

Use your breath to check in and your voice to have your say!

You see there's so much joy to be had. It's life's true essence!

Just remember Evie's secrets of **gratitude, connection, kindness, uniqueness** and most importantly **presence!**

Printed in Great Britain
by Amazon

28594383R00021